all the magic!
Tabatha Jean D'Agata

D1709966

MORE WISHES

Written by
Tabatha Jean D'Agata

Illustrated by
Alex Goubar

ISBN: 9781989506783

Published in Canada by Pandamonium Publishing House™.
www.pandamoniumpublishing.com

Design: Alex Goubar
Cover Design: Alex Goubar
alexgoubar.com

Because of Helen

For Connor, Calvin & Carter

Ladybug on your hand.
Watch its wings expand.
Make a wish.
Flutter! Flutter! Flutter!
Will your wish come true?

Pick a dandelion and blow
its puff of seeds.
Make a wish.
Fly! Fly! Fly!
Will your wish come true?

Paper lantern high in the sky.
Make a wish.
Up! Up! Up!
Will your wish come true?

Pick a four-leaf clover.
Make a wish.
Toss! Toss! Toss!
Will your wish come true?

Eyelash on your cheek,
now on your fingertip.
Make a wish.
Blow! Blow! Blow!
Will your wish come true?

Leaf falling from a tree.
Make a wish.
Catch! Catch! Catch!
Will your wish come true?

Put a penny in your left shoe. Make a wish.
Skip! Skip! Skip! Will your wish come true?

Coin in a wishing well.
Make a wish. Plop! Plop! Plop!
Will your wish come true?

Jump seven waves along the ocean shore.
Make a wish. Splash! Splash! Splash!
Will your wish come true?

Shooting star across the moon.
Make a wish. Zoom! Zoom! Zoom!
Will your wish come true?

Tie a ribbon on the tree.
Make a wish. Dream! Dream! Dream!
Will your wish come true?

See a rainbow. Close your eyes and count to ten.
Make a wish. Luck! Luck! Luck!
Will your wish come true?

Fireworks paint the dark.
Make a wish. Pop! Pop! Pop!
Will your wish come true?

A birthday cake to celebrate.
Make a wish. Poof! Poof! Poof!
Will your wish come true?

Children around the world have different ways to
wish, and not every wish that's wished for will come
true. So, keep this in mind, every wishing time,
if you don't get what you wish for
there is something you can do.

KEEP MAKING MORE WISHES!

Now which wish will you choose?

MORE WISHES

Wishing cultures: myths, folklores, superstitions, and traditions.

A FALLING LEAF

If you see a falling leaf and catch it before it hits the ground your wish will come true. This appears to have originated in London, though it's not clearly documented. (Other traditions also suggest writing your wish on a fallen leaf.)

PENNY IN SHOE

Find a penny, pick it up, and all day long you'll have good luck!
This practice was taught to me by my grandmother. Find a penny, make a wish, and put it in your shoe so it will come true. The belief of a penny being lucky dates back to ancient Rome but is well-known in many countries.

WISHING ON AN EYELASH

This folklore has been around since the 19th century and originates from the UK, particularly Britain and England. If you wish on a fallen eyelash by blowing it the wish will come true.

WISHING WELL

Another well-known tradition with a European origin. Make a wish and toss a coin into a well and your wish will come true.

WISHING TREE

In Turkey people tie strips of cloth, string, or ribbon on wishing trees to make wishes.

PAPER LANTERN

In Asia paper lanterns are used to send a wish into the sky during cultural festivals and celebrations. Water lanterns are also used.

BIRTHDAY CANDLE

Making a wish and blowing out the birthday candle is a staple tradition all over the world. Its origin is believed to have started in Greece with Ancient Greeks.

LADYBUG

The belief across many cultures is that if a ladybug lands on you and you make a wish it will carry your wish away and it will come true. They are also known in Europe and in the UK as lady beetles or ladybirds.

FOUR-LEAF CLOVER

A long known Irish legend (Celtic groups) that picking a four-leaf clover was good luck or wishing upon it would make the wish come true.

DANDELION

This tradition is well-known all over the world. It's my absolute favorite! I can't resist making a dandelion wish when I see one! Pick a dandelion, make a wish while blowing all the white fluffy seeds off a dandelion head and your wish will come true.

About the author

Tabatha Jean D'Agata was a redheaded, freckled-faced kid born in Lawrence, Massachusetts. Her love for creating stories and characters began at a young age. D'Agata has authored several children's books and is a longtime literacy columnist for the Parent Express Newspaper. Aside from writing, she especially enjoys spending time with her family and making memories with her grandsons (including her German Shepherd grandson named Mocha). Tabatha currently resides in Hooksett, NH where you'll often find her putting a penny in her shoe for good luck and blowing dandelion wishes.

Alex Goubar is a digital illustrator who has completed
her Bachelor's Degree in Illustration at Sheridan College.
She had begun her children's book illustrating adventure
during her 3rd year co-op, where Lacey invited her to join
her team. Alex was born in Minsk, Belarus and is currently
living in Ontario, Canada.

www.alexgoubar.com
@goub_art

For more fabulous titles
visit
www.pandamoniumpublishing.com

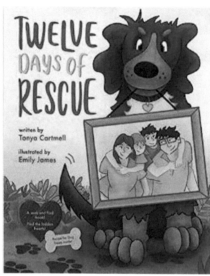

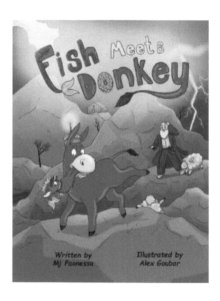

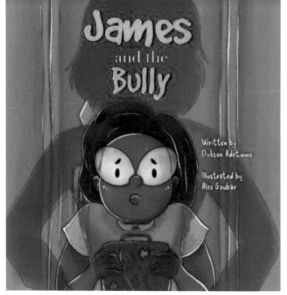

Printed in the USA
CPSIA information can be obtained
at www.ICGtesting.com
LVHW061929201123
764445LV00002B/81